Start to sign!

The Royal National Institute for Deaf People

Start to sign!

Richard Magill

Anne Hodgson

The Royal National Institute for Deaf People

Published by

The Royal National Institute for Deaf People (RNID)
19-23 Featherstone Street, London EC1Y 8SL

First published 2000
Second edition 2001

Printed in Great Britain by Blackmore Ltd.

ISBN 0 900634 73 1 paperback 1st edition
ISBN 0 900634 84 7 paperback 2nd edition

The handshape illustrations used in this publication are reproduced with the permission of the Deaf Studies Research Unit, University of Durham. The handshape illustrations are taken from the *Dictionary of British Sign Language/English* (Faber and Faber, 1992). The dictionary was produced by the Deaf Studies Research Unit for the British Deaf Association.

Contents

Acknowledgements

This book would not have been possible without the involvement of many people.

The models were RNID staff: Celal Djemal, Helen Ellis, Roz German, Barbara Laumets, Angela Miller, Asha Nauth, Sara Olsen, Sally Paull, Siân Smith and Rebecca Tadman.

Particular thanks go to Sally Paull and Linda Richards who made time in their busy schedules to comment on the text at different stages. Thanks also go to Robert Farquharson, Rosanna Preston, Bob Wray, Susannah Calderan, Kathryn Merritt, Stefanie Hafner and the interpreters who supported us.

RNID's Publications Team looked after the project as a whole: Yael Hodder, Julie Labourdette and Suzanne Mullins were the designers, Lynn Jackson was editor, and Bridget Middleton and Philippa Smart were project managers.

Jens Storch was our photographer and Jennie Dooge was responsible for the layout.

Thanks also go to David Brien of the University of Durham for many helpful suggestions and to Clive Mason for the foreword.

Foreword by Clive Mason

As a user of British Sign Language, I am delighted to see this new edition of *Start to Sign!* More people start learning to sign every year and this book aims to help and encourage anyone who is taking sign language classes by reinforcing what you will learn, and providing a source of reference.

Many people start learning to sign for their own interest. Others learn because they know someone who is deaf, or because they have contact with deaf people at work. In addition to covering much of the vocabulary you need for everyday conversations, the book provides basic information about the grammar of BSL. BSL is not a translation of English – in fact there are signs that are very difficult to express in English at all – but a language in its own right, the language of the Deaf Community in Britain. Through BSL you will have the opportunity to learn about the Deaf Community and experience the richness and variety of Deaf Culture.

Clive Mason is an active member of the Deaf Community who campaigns for Deaf rights. His love of language led him to work in the media field, and he presented the BBC's See Hear programme for many years, after which he lectured at Wolverhampton University. He currently works for Independent Media Support Limited, providing in-vision-signing access on Digital TV.

Preface to the second edition

We are delighted to be revising and reprinting *Start to sign!* just a year after it was first published. This has provided us with the opportunity to amend and expand it.

Various sections in the introductory text have been revised and expanded for greater clarity.

The photographs include a new section on communication (pages 159 to 160), and we have added new photographs to other sections: 'write' and 'portable textphone' on page 143, 'crisis' on page 144, and 'Typetalk' on page 142. These are all signs that we feel are important for anyone starting to learn BSL. Additionally, we have made a few amendments to the directional arrows and handshapes shown with the photographs.

We would like to thank all those colleagues and members of the Deaf Community who contributed comments and suggestions on the first edition, in particular Penny Beschizza and Judith Jackson.

Introduction to British Sign Language

History

We can probably assume that sign language has been around for as long as there have been deaf people who wanted to communicate. First records of British Sign Language (BSL) date from the 16th century; there are even earlier records of sign language in other countries. BSL was used in schools for deaf children and learned by increasing numbers of people until the end of the last century. Then in 1880, at a conference in Milan, a group of teachers working with deaf children – who believed the teaching of sign language was detrimental to the acquisition of spoken language – voted that sign language should no longer be taught in schools. This decision affected several European countries. In England it meant that only spoken and written English were taught, and that use of BSL in schools was actively discouraged. This 'Oral Method' remained dominant for almost 100 years. However, in 1979, Conrad's book *The Deaf School Child* revealed that profoundly deaf children were leaving school at 16 with an average reading age of less than nine. From this time, attitudes towards the use of BSL with deaf children in schools began to change and become more positive.

Over the last 20 years, BSL has gained a great deal in popularity and influence. It is frequently seen on television, both when programmes use sign language interpreters to give sign language users access to them, and in programmes that are specifically targeted at deaf people. An increase in the numbers of Deaf people training as BSL tutors has led to the establishment of BSL classes all over the UK. More and more people are learning to sign and over 100,000 people have passed their Stage I (Basic) examination in BSL.

BSL today

How many people use BSL today? It is hard to be sure for two reasons:

Firstly, BSL is the language of the British Deaf Community. It is used by many people who are born deaf and learn to sign as children, BSL being

their first language. However, only one deaf child in 10 has deaf parents, so there are many deaf people who learn BSL as their second language, after having learnt English. Some of these people describe BSL as their *preferred* language. Lots of deaf children learn BSL at school.

Secondly, some deaf people do not use BSL, but Sign Supported English, or SSE. SSE is not a language in its own right, independent of English, but more a kind of English with signs. Many people you see signing may be using SSE. Other people use neither BSL nor SSE, but elements of each, so that their signing is somewhere between the two. For this reason it is hard to give an exact figure for the number of sign language users. It is thought that, of the 8.7 million people in the UK with some degree of hearing loss, about 50,000 sign.

The Deaf Community and Deaf Culture

BSL users are also members of the Deaf Community. They describe themselves as Deaf, written with a capital 'D' to emphasise their Deaf identity, take part in Deaf events, and may attend Deaf Clubs and groups. Deaf people believe strongly in their right to participate fully and equally in society.

How to learn BSL and find classes

Nobody can learn BSL just from a book, or even from a video or CD-ROM. These are useful back-up resources if you want to remind yourself of signs, or practise at home, but the only way to learn BSL is from a Deaf person, ideally from a qualified BSL tutor.

Qualifications in BSL are at five levels; the first level is called Stage I. Curricula and examinations are set by the Council for the Advancement of Communication with Deaf People (CACDP). CACDP's address is on page 209. CACDP has a Tutor Policy, which sets out the recommended standards for BSL tutors. If you want to learn BSL and have not already found a sign language class, you can get details of courses in your area from the RNID Information Line, tel: 0808 808 0123; textphone: 0808 808 9000; fax: 020 7296 8199; e-mail: informationline@rnid.org.uk

Popular myths

There are many misconceptions about sign language.

Sign language is not international; BSL is used only in Britain. Each country has its own sign language, although some sign languages are closely related to one another. American Sign Language and French Sign Language share similar roots, although they are now separate languages. Auslan (Australian Sign Language) and BSL are very similar.

BSL is not an 'invented' language, such as Esperanto. It evolved naturally as languages do. Like any language it has its own grammar and syntax. It can express anything that its users want to say and if there is no sign to express a particular idea, BSL users will develop one, in the same way that speakers of English form new words to describe new concepts. Examples of very new signs in BSL are the signs for *Internet* and *e-mail*. Both *Internet* and *e-mail* are new words in English too.

It is very important to remember that, since BSL is a language in its own right, you cannot translate English into BSL, word for sign. Some English words or phrases have no direct translation into BSL, and some signs have no direct translation into English. As you learn more BSL you will understand the meanings of signs used from the context in which you see them, rather than by associating them with any English word. Examples of signs that are particularly difficult to put into English are multi-channel signs. There is more information about these on page 16.

Regional variation

Like spoken languages, BSL has many regional variations. For example, we show a numbering system on pages 200-203, but it is very possible that you will learn a different system at your BSL class. Colours are another group of signs with many regional variants. If you move about then it is useful to learn and remember different regional signs. You may find that the signs you learn are not always the same as the ones in this book. If you move from one part of the country to another, you may find that some of your signs have different meanings, or that you learn a second sign for something.

Left-handed people

The photographs in this book are of right-handed signing. If you are left-handed, you should use your left hand where our photographs show someone signing with their right hand. Where they use their left hand, you should use your right hand. Movements from one side to the other should be made in the opposite direction to that shown in the photographs. When you read the section on time lines, remember that the information we have given is for right-handed people, and that if you are left-handed you should place the time lines on the opposite side of your body.

The components of the language

Until they watch it closely, or begin to learn it themselves, most people think that BSL is just a series of gestures. In fact, it is far more complex than that. We can identify four basic components:

Handshape: how you hold your fingers and thumbs.

Movement: of your hand through a defined space.

Non-manual features (NMFs): facial expression and shoulder movement.

Spatial orientation: the relationship of the hand to the signer's body.

Structure

In English, a sentence is controlled by the verb; other parts of the sentence are organised in relation to it. The meaning of the sentence is often dependent on the position of other words in relation to the verb.

BSL is structured in a completely different way, and to learn it you must disregard what you know about English grammar because it is not relevant. In BSL, the first thing you sign in any utterance is usually the main subject, or topic. After that you define the subject by commenting on it. The sentence 'What is your name?' in English would therefore appear in BSL as:

you → name → what?

 lipshape (questioning expression)

This structure, which is completely unlike the structure of English, is used by some spoken languages too.

Directional verbs

One feature of BSL is that some of its verbs can change direction. We have indicated these *directional verbs* throughout this book by putting **DV** under the photographs, but the pictures below give an example of how one of these verbs works. You can use the sign 'ask' by moving your hand from a position near to yourself towards someone to mean *'I ask you'* or *'I am asking you'*. If you use the same sign but begin it with your hand about 40 cm away and move it towards yourself that means *'you are asking me'* or *'you ask me'*. You can use the same sign to mean *he/she/you/they ask(s) you/him/her/them'* by moving your hand from one 'person' or group of people in the defined signing space in front of you to another.

I am asking you

Modification

Signs modify to add meaning. The three photographs below all use the sign for *raining*. NMFs – and in real life, how much you stress the signs – all show how heavy the rain is.

Light rain or drizzle

Heavier rain

Pouring with rain

The signing space

BSL users sign in a clearly defined space, which starts a little below waist level and goes up to a few centimetres above their head. It stretches to arm's length in front of them. The use of this space is extremely important to the meaning of what is signed.

Placement

Someone using BSL to describe something they have seen will situate all the components within the space in front of them at elbow height. They will first define the area – for example a room, field or road – and will then place items or actions inside that space, in precise relation to the confines of the space and what they are describing, as they visualise it, not as a mirror image. They may use their gaze to emphasise the placement of components within the space.

Iconicity

Some signs seem to look like the idea they represent. For example, if you look at the photograph of the sign for 'crab' on page 23, you can see it looks like a crab. The sign for 'sew' looks like someone sewing. This feature is called 'iconicity' or 'visual motivation'. These signs are not miming; they work within the grammar of BSL and conform to its rules. Many signs have this visual connection with their meaning – and many do not.

Time lines

Time is positioned around the body of the signer by means of one of four time lines:

- To our right, between waist and shoulder level, is a time line that indicates age, usually of children.

- A time line over the right shoulder indicates time on a large and general scale, from recently to years ago (see page 194 for 'long ago' and page 196 for 'recently').

- A time line along the left arm and hand shows precise time, measured in weeks.

- A time line that runs in front of you from left to right at elbow level shows continuous time.

Compound signs

Sometimes two signs together are used to make another meaning. Examples of these are 'decide' (page 179) and 'believe' (page 180).

Multi-channel signs

Multi-channel signs cannot easily be translated into English. They use more than one channel, for example a sign, movement and specific NMFs. They rarely have a direct equivalent in English and often it takes a whole phrase or more to capture the meaning of a multi-channel sign in English. Below is one example of a multi-channel sign, meaning 'I am not bothered'.

Lip patterns

Never forget that lip patterns are a very important part of BSL. The pictures for 'aunt', 'uncle', 'niece' and 'nephew' on page 105 illustrate this. The handshape and movement are the same for all four signs, but the lip pattern is different in each case.

Sign names

Deaf sign language users are often given sign names. Your BSL teacher will probably give you one. There are different kinds of sign names, for example a sign that shows:

- A physical feature of the person – such as a hairstyle.

- A characteristic, such as being fidgety or having a quick temper.

- A translation or pun on the person's English first name or surname, such as Dawn, Penny or Rose, Brown, Forest or Walker.

Some people fingerspell their initials, particularly if their first and second names begin with the same letter. For example, Sam Smith would be SS. People with a short first name such as Mel, Rob or Pam may just fingerspell it.

Here are some examples of sign names:

Richard was given his sign name at school. He was at school in Yorkshire where the sign for 11 is the sign shown in the second picture. Richard's name was number 11 on the register and he also had a habit of rubbing his nose. His sign name, shown in the first picture is a combination of these two things.

Sally's sign name is her initials, SP, fingerspelled. There is more information about fingerspelling below.

Rebecca's sign name is a mannerism; she pushes her hair behind her ears.

Fingerspelling

All letters of the English alphabet can be spelled on your hands. This alphabet – the manual alphabet or fingerspelling – is used to spell out the names of people or places that do not have sign names.

Some signs are developed from fingerspelling. For example, in parts of Britain, fingerspelled letters are used for days of the week. M spelled twice quickly is Monday, T twice is Tuesday, W twice is Wednesday; for Thursday spell Th once. Only Friday, Saturday and Sunday have specific signs and the sign for Friday has developed from the fingerspelled F.

How to understand the photographs

Looking at the photographs

As we said earlier, it is impossible to learn to sign from a book. However, we do hope that you will find the photographs in this book a useful guide to refer to while you are taking a course in BSL.

Below is the photograph of the sign for 'autumn'. The English meaning is written below the photograph. The diagram in the top right-hand corner of the photograph shows exactly the handshape you should make. Where you use both hands to make the sign, and need a different handshape for each, we have shown both handshapes. Right-handed people should use the handshape in the top of each photograph for their right hand. If there is another handshape diagram below it, that is the handshape for the left hand. If you are left-handed, reverse them. The red line with an arrow shows the direction in which your hand should move, and how it should move. For example, for this sign your hands should both move downwards in a wavy pattern from left to right.

If there are two handshapes shown, but the sign is made with one hand, that means your handshape changes during the sign.

There is extra information underneath some photographs. The letters **DV,** for example, mean that the word is a directional verb (see page 13 for more information). Occasionally we have added a few words to clarify the meaning of a sign.

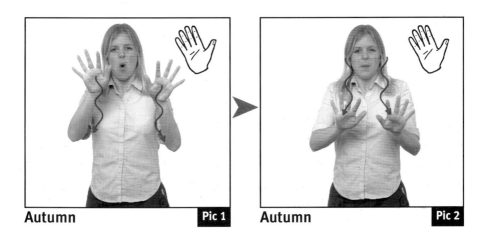

Autumn `Pic 1` **Autumn** `Pic 2`

Pairs or groups of photographs that illustrate one sign

In many cases we have used more than one photograph to illustrate a sign. Where we have done this, there is a triangular arrow between the photographs, and they are labelled 'Pic 1', 'Pic 2', 'Pic 3', and so on. Examples of this are 'jacket' on page 32 and 'Italy' on page 38.

Photographs of alternative signs for the same English word

BSL has many regional variations and it is common for there to be more than one sign with the same meaning. We have not illustrated all of the signs for each English word, but where two different signs are frequently used, we have shown both of them. Where this has happened, we have labelled the photographs 'A' and 'B'. Examples of this are 'kind' on page 162 and 'before' on page 193.

The signs

Animal

Bird

Fish

Butterfly

Spider

Crab

Dog

Cat

Mouse

Rabbit

Horse

Donkey

Pig

Hen

Sheep

Cow

Deer

Camel

Lion Pic 1

Lion Pic 2

Elephant Pic 1

Elephant Pic 2

Snake Pic 1

Snake Pic 2

Colour

Orange

Red

Brown

Yellow `Pic 1`

Yellow `Pic 2`

27

Black

Blue

Green

Pink

White `Pic 1`

White `Pic 2`

Gold Pic 1 Gold Pic 2

Silver Pic 1 Silver Pic 2

Clothes

Hat

Shoe Pic 1

Shoe Pic 2

Sandal Pic 1

Sandal Pic 2

Boots

Socks

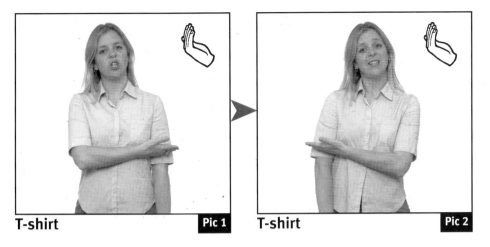

T-shirt Pic 1 **T-shirt** Pic 2

Jeans

Skirt

Miniskirt A

Miniskirt B

Dress

Shirt

Jacket Pic 1

Jacket Pic 2

Tie

Shorts

Jumper — Pic 1 · **Jumper** — Pic 2

Deaf · **Hard of hearing**

Deafened — Pic 1 · **Deafened** — Pic 2

Hearing

Hearing aid

Sign language `Pic 1`

Sign language `Pic 2`

Lipread DV

Blind

Usher Syndrome `Pic 1`

Usher Syndrome `Pic 2`

Disabled `Pic 1`

Disabled `Pic 2`

Britain

England

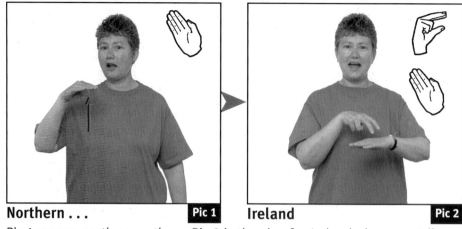

Northern ... `Pic 1` **Ireland** `Pic 2`

Pic 1 means *north* or *northern*. Pic 2 is the sign for *Ireland* when you talk about *Northern Ireland*. The sign for the *Republic of Ireland* is on page 37.

Scotland

Wales

Countries

Europe

Republic of Ireland `Pic 1` **Republic of Ireland** `Pic 2`

The sign for *Northern Ireland* is on page 36.

Sweden `Pic 1` **Sweden** `Pic 2`

Norway **Denmark**

Russia — Pic 1

Russia — Pic 2

France

Germany

Italy — Pic 1

Italy — Pic 2

Greece

India

Spain `Pic 1`

Spain `Pic 2`

Portugal `Pic 1`

Portugal `Pic 2`

Africa — Pic 1

Africa — Pic 2

Australia — Pic 1

Australia — Pic 2

New... — Pic 1

...Zealand — Pic 2

China

United States of America

Japan　Pic 1

Japan　Pic 2

Breakfast

Toast

Bacon

Egg

Milk Pic 1

Milk Pic 2

Cereal

Ice cream

Cake

Biscuit

Bread

Sandwich

Chocolate

Café

Spoon

Knife

Fork

Menu

Salt/pepper

Glass

Plate

Bowl

Hot (food) Pic 1 **Hot (food)** Pic 2

Sweet

Bitter

Dinner/restaurant

Soup

Fish (to eat)

Meat

Salad

Pudding

Fruit

Apple

Cherries `Pic 1`

Cherries `Pic 2`

Banana

Melon

Peach

Vegetable

Tomato

Onion

Potato

Carrot

Pea `Pic 1`

Pea `Pic 2`

Pasta `Pic 1`

Pasta `Pic 2`

Rice

Chicken

Chips

Cheese

Picnic Pic 1 **Picnic** Pic 2

Ice Pic 1 **Ice** Pic 2

Cream — Pic 1

Cream — Pic 2

Sugar

Jam

Butter — Pic 1

Butter — Pic 2

Nuts

Drink

Coffee

Tea

Wine

Beer

Whisky `Pic 1`

Whisky `Pic 2`

Healthy `Pic 1`

Healthy `Pic 2`

Ill

Cough

Flu/cold

Pain

Vomit

Doctor

Dentist

Nurse

Emergency

Hospital

Tablet `Pic 1`

Tablet `Pic 2`

Medicine

Operation

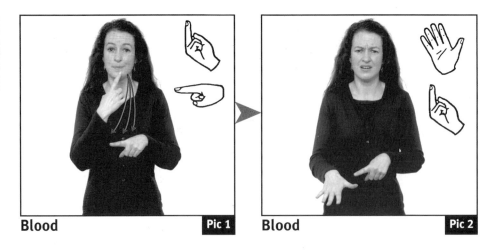

Blood `Pic 1` **Blood** `Pic 2`

Heart

Accident

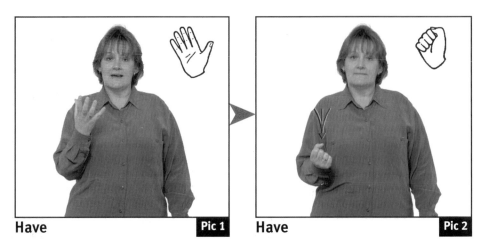

Have `Pic 1` **Have** `Pic 2`

Lend/borrow DV — Pic 1 **Lend/borrow DV** — Pic 2

This sign starts from the person lending and moves towards the person borrowing.

Keep

Buy

Sell — Pic 1 **Sell** — Pic 2

Home

Go home

Address

House

Garden/park

Flower

Tree

Lawn

Rubbish Pic 1

Rubbish Pic 2

Neighbour Pic 1

Neighbour Pic 2

59

Dirty — Pic 1

Dirty — Pic 2

Bath

Soap

Water

Toothbrush

Bed

Blanket

Duvet

Curtains

Wake up `Pic 1`

Wake up `Pic 2`

61

Go to sleep — Pic 1

Go to sleep — Pic 2

Asleep

Door

Chain — Pic 1

Chain — Pic 2

Wall Pic 1

Wall Pic 2

Window Pic 1

Window Pic 2

Corner

Kitchen

Table/flat
Either a flat surface, or a flat to live in.

Chair

Cupboard Pic 1

Cupboard Pic 2

Refrigerator Pic 1

Refrigerator Pic 2

Cooker

Washing machine

Sink `Pic 1`

Sink `Pic 2`

Toilet

Decorating

65

Sweep

Scrub

Sitting room `Pic 1`

Sitting room `Pic 2`

Armchair

Carpet

Radio

Sofa

Hall Pic 1

Hall Pic 2

Attic Pic 1

Attic Pic 2

Stairs

Electricity

Gas

Lights

Money

Pound

Penny `Pic 1`

Penny `Pic 2`

Euro `A Pic 1`

Euro `A Pic 2`

Euro `B`

Dollar

69

Expensive | A Pic 1

Expensive | A Pic 2

Expensive | B

Cheap

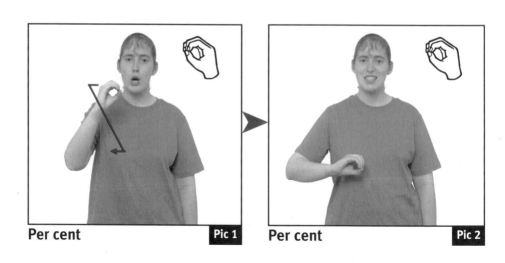

Per cent | Pic 1

Per cent | Pic 2

Bank

Insurance

Spend Pic 1

Spend Pic 2

Save Pic 1

Save Pic 2

Walk — Pic 1

Walk — Pic 2

Run — Pic 1

Run — Pic 2

Jump — A

Jump — B

Fall Pic 1

Fall Pic 2

Dive

Stand

Sit

Kneel

Lead/guide Pic 1

Lead/guide Pic 2

Follow

Lie down

Place/area

London/noise

74

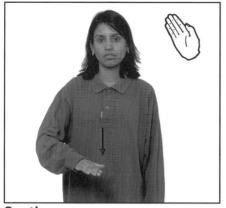

South

The sign for *north* is on page 36.

East

West

On (as in *on top of*)

Over (as in *above*) `Pic 1`

Over (as in *above*) `Pic 2`

Under

Outside

Inside `Pic 1` **Inside** `Pic 2`

Sea

Beach

Island

Forest

Town

Village

Valley

Hill

Road

River

Lake

Mountain

Question

Ask DV (see also page 13)

Answer Pic 1

Answer Pic 2

Who

What

How

When

Where

Why/because

Reason

Which

How many? Pic 1

How many? Pic 2

Polite Pic 1

Polite Pic 2

Rude

Hello

Please Pic 1

Please Pic 2

Thank you — Pic 1

Thank you — Pic 2

Excuse me — Pic 1

Excuse me — Pic 2

How are you? — Pic 1

How are you? — Pic 2

Sorry

Goodbye

Sport `Pic 1`

Sport `Pic 2`

Golf `Pic 1`

Golf `Pic 2`

Badminton

Tennis

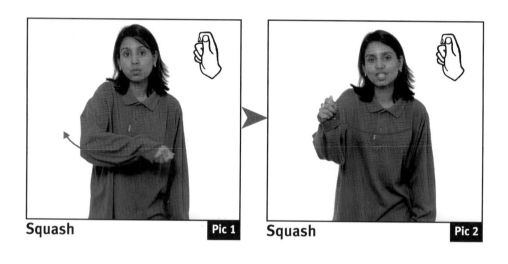

Squash `Pic 1`

Squash `Pic 2`

Cricket `Pic 1`

Cricket `Pic 2`

Rugby `Pic 1`

Rugby `Pic 2`

Ball

Football

Goal

Referee

Crowd

Horse riding

Cycling

Sailing

Boat

Skiing

Cinema

Film

Theatre

Play (at the theatre)

Actor

Bar/pub

Dance — Pic 1

Dance — Pic 2

Bottle — Pic 1

Bottle — Pic 2

Sing — Pic 1

Sing — Pic 2

Party

Drunk

Knit

Sew

Paint Pic 1

Paint Pic 2

89

Sewing machine

Camera/photograph

Photograph (snapshot)

Dream/imagine

See DV `A Pic 1`

See DV `A Pic 2`

I look at you B

You look at me B

Lazy

Rest

Relax Pic 1

Relax Pic 2

Play (a game)

Competition

Cheat `Pic 1`

Cheat `Pic 2`

Win `Pic 1`

Win `Pic 2`

Lose Pic 1

Lose Pic 2

Programme

Video recorder

Video tape A

Video tape B

93

Record (from television) **A Pic 1**

Record (from television) **A Pic 2**

Record (music) **B Pic 1**

Record (music) **B Pic 2**

Television **Pic 1**

Television **Pic 2**

Queue Pic 1 **Queue** Pic 2

Book (reserve)

Shop

Ticket

Birthday

Read

Book (to read)

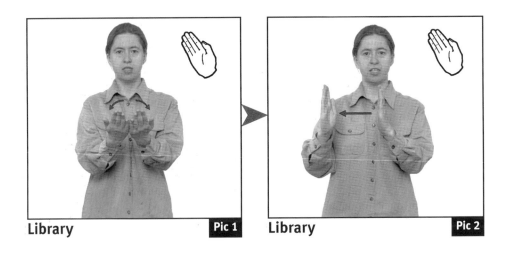

Library Pic 1

Library Pic 2

Newspaper Pic 1

Newspaper Pic 2

Tell a story DV Pic 1 Tell a story DV Pic 2

Music Pic 1 Music Pic 2

Help DV Pic 1 Help DV Pic 2

Association — Pic 1

Association — Pic 2

Community

Volunteer

Organise — Pic 1

Organise — Pic 2

Charity **Pic 1**

Charity **Pic 2**

Few

Plenty

Lots **Pic 1**

Lots **Pic 2**

Nothing

Quarter

Half

Number

First

Second

Third

Weigh

Measure `Pic 1`

Measure `Pic 2`

I

You (he/she/it)
This sign means you, he, she or it,
depending on whom you point to.

My

Mine

The sign for *your* or *yours*, is made in the same way but the knuckles and palm of your hand face the person you are talking to.

Myself `Pic 1`

Myself `Pic 2`

Family

Husband/wife

People

Father

Mother `Pic 1` **Mother** `Pic 2`

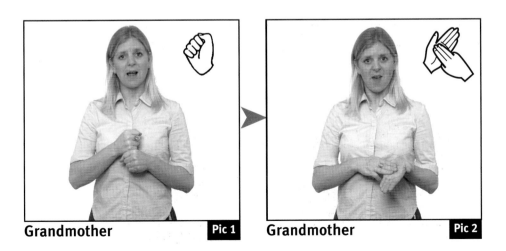

Grandmother `Pic 1` **Grandmother** `Pic 2`

Grandfather — Pic 1 Grandfather — Pic 2

Brother

Sister

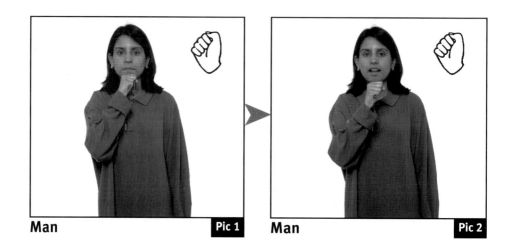

Man — Pic 1 Man — Pic 2

Woman

Child

Uncle

Aunt

Nephew

Niece

Son

Daughter

Cousin `Pic 1` **Cousin** `Pic 2`

Person

Meet `A`

Meet · B Pic 1

Meet · B Pic 2

Introduce · Pic 1

Introduce · Pic 2

Single · Pic 1

Single · Pic 2

Friend

Gay

Lesbian

Born

Die

Boy

Girl

Baby

Grow up

Name

Marry `Pic 1`

Marry `Pic 2`

Divorce Pic 1

Divorce Pic 2

Queen/King

Government

Prime Minister Pic 1

Prime Minister Pic 2

Party (political)

Council

Educate `Pic 1`

Educate `Pic 2`

Teach DV

Training

Know

Clear

Confused

Slow down!

Learn `Pic 1`

Learn `Pic 2`

Forget Pic 1

Forget Pic 2

Lesson A

Lesson B

School

Encourage

Understand Pic 1

Understand Pic 2

Over my head Pic 1

Over my head Pic 2

Attention

Confident

College

Degree/diploma

Lose confidence

Gallaudet . . . `Pic 1`

Gallaudet . . . `Pic 2`

. . . University `Pic 3`

Lecture

Stupid (person)

Intelligent `Pic 1`

Intelligent `Pic 2`

Average `Pic 1`

Average `Pic 2`

Exams `Pic 1`

Exams `Pic 2`

Fail `Pic 1`

Fail `Pic 2`

Pass

Defer/put off

Traffic

Car

Coach

Bus

Engine

Drive

Caravan

Petrol

Crash `Pic 1`

Crash `Pic 2`

Train/railway

Helicopter

Aeroplane

Foreign/abroad

Far away

Language

Holiday Pic 1

Holiday Pic 2

Hotel `Pic 1` **Hotel** `Pic 2`

Sunbathe `Pic 1` **Sunbathe** `Pic 2`

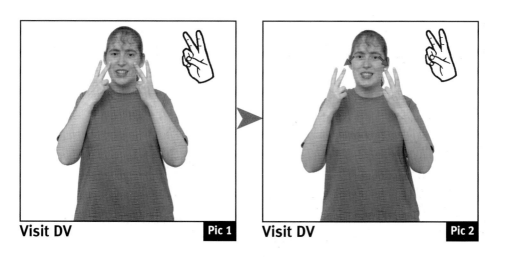

Visit DV `Pic 1` **Visit DV** `Pic 2`

Plan — Pic 1 **Plan** — Pic 2

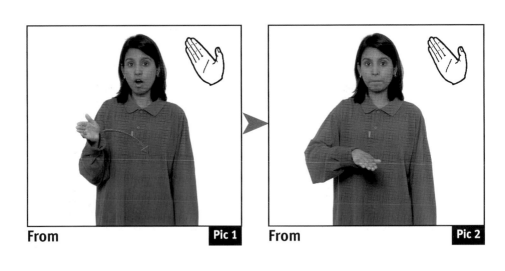

From — Pic 1 **From** — Pic 2

Go DV — Pic 1 **Go DV** — Pic 2

Between

Arrive

Come `Pic 1`

Come `Pic 2`

Way `Pic 1`

Way `Pic 2`

Travel

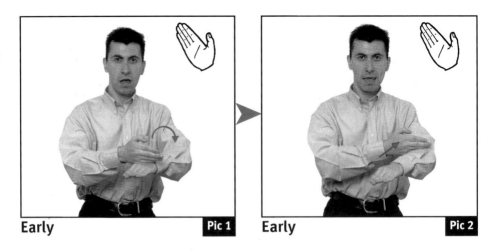

Early — Pic 1 **Early** — Pic 2

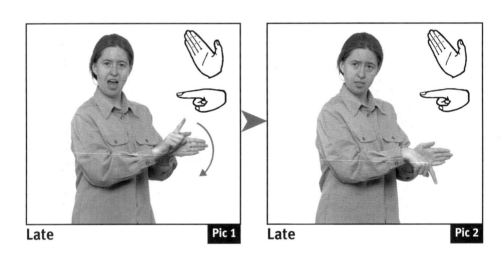

Late — Pic 1 **Late** — Pic 2

Weather

Sun

Hot `Pic 1`

Hot `Pic 2`

Cloud

Thunder/lightning

Rain

Cool

125

Cold

Snow

Windy Pic 1

Windy Pic 2

Fog

Gale

Steal Pic 1

Steal Pic 2

Burglar

Fine (money)

Murder

Prison

127

Escape Pic 1 **Escape** Pic 2

Law Pic 1 **Law** Pic 2

Suspicious DV

Fight

Proof

Guilty

Solicitor A Pic 1

Solicitor A Pic 2

Solicitor B

Judge

Barrister Pic 1 **Barrister** Pic 2

Police Pic 1 **Police** Pic 2

Detective

Court

Space

World

Moon A

Moon B

Star

Spaceship

Sunday

Monday

Tuesday `Pic 1`

Tuesday `Pic 2`

Wednesday `Pic 1`

Wednesday `Pic 2`

Thursday `Pic 1` **Thursday** `Pic 2`

Friday

Saturday

Weekend `Pic 1` **Weekend** `Pic 2`

133

Week Pic 1 **Week** Pic 2

Fortnight Pic 1 **Fortnight** Pic 2

Day Pic 1 **Day** Pic 2

Month

Afternoon

Morning Pic 1

Morning Pic 2

Evening

Night

Yesterday Pic 1 Yesterday Pic 2

Today

Ages ago

Tomorrow Pic 1

Tomorrow Pic 2

Last week **Pic 1**

Last week **Pic 2**

Next week

Future

Past **Pic 1**

Past **Pic 2**

Spring Pic 1

Spring Pic 2

Autumn Pic 1

Autumn Pic 2

Summer

Winter

Christmas — Pic 1 Christmas — Pic 2

Easter

Diary

Three o'clock — Pic 1 Three o'clock — Pic 2

By holding up the right number of fingers and making the same hand movement, you can sign other times.

139

Half... **Pic 1**

...past... **Pic 2**

...three **Pic 3**

Time

Wristwatch

Clock

Remember **Pic 1** Remember **Pic 2**

Remind **Pic 1** Remind **Pic 2**

Work Office

Telephone DV

Telephone DV

Textphone

Videophone

Typetalk Pic 1

Typetalk Pic 2

Portable textphone

Write

Envelope

Internet `Pic 1`

Internet `Pic 2`

Internet `Pic 3`

E-mail `Pic 1`

E-mail `Pic 2`

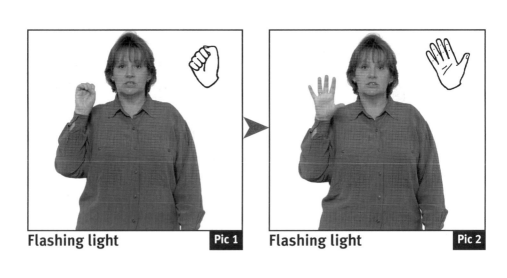

Flashing light `Pic 1`

Flashing light `Pic 2`

Crisis `Pic 1`

Crisis `Pic 2`

Computer — Pic 1 Computer — Pic 2

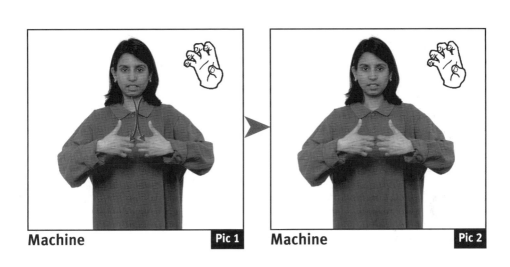

Machine — Pic 1 Machine — Pic 2

Paper — Pic 1 Paper — Pic 2

Letter Pic 1

Letter Pic 2

Print Pic 1

Print Pic 2

Fax (to someone) DV

Fax (from someone) DV

Photocopier `Pic 1` **Photocopier** `Pic 2`

Employer

Employee

Advertise

Administration

Redundant `Pic 1`

Redundant `Pic 2`

Dismiss `Pic 1`

Dismiss `Pic 2`

Unemployed `Pic 1`

Unemployed `Pic 2`

148

Meeting `Pic 1`

Meeting `Pic 2`

Research `Pic 1`

Research `Pic 2`

Agenda

Delegate

Committee

Fireman

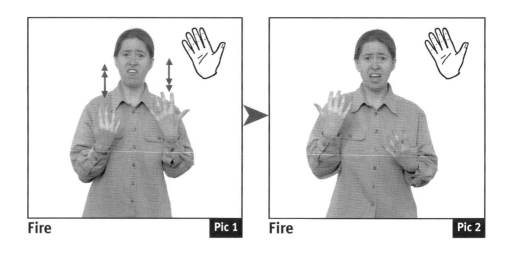

Fire Pic 1

Fire Pic 2

Engineer

Farmer

Soldier Pic 1

Soldier Pic 2

Sailor Pic 1

Sailor Pic 2

Service Pic 1

Service Pic 2

Profit

Salary

Accounts

Benefit

Strike Pic 1

Strike Pic 2

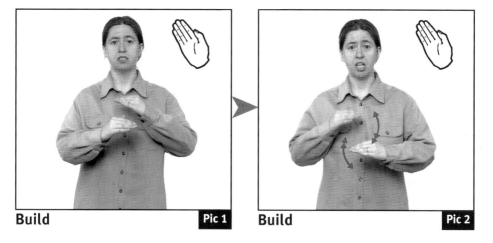

Build — Pic 1 Build — Pic 2

Factory

Make

Metal

Wood

153

Repair

Busy

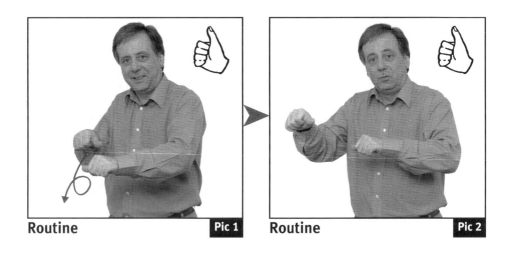

Routine `Pic 1`

Routine `Pic 2`

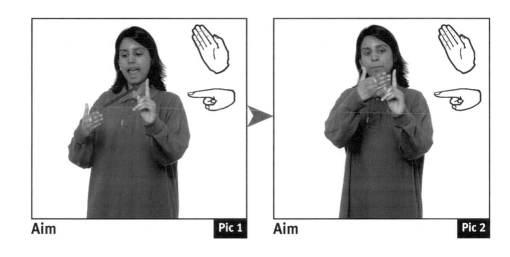

Aim `Pic 1`

Aim `Pic 2`

Experience `Pic 1` **Experience** `Pic 2`

Control

Depend

Responsible

Improve

155

Concentrate

Analyse

Hard/difficult

Easy

Use

Arrange

Establish

Mistake

Danger

Safety

Communicate

Typing

Begin `Pic 1` **Begin** `Pic 2`

Finish

Ready

Deadline `Pic 1` **Deadline** `Pic 2`

SpeedText `Pic 1`

SpeedText `Pic 2`

Videophone

Interpreter

Lipspeaker `Pic 1`

Lipspeaker `Pic 2`

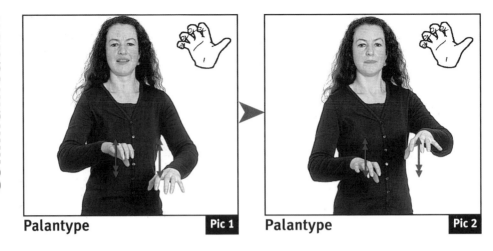

Palantype — Pic 1

Palantype — Pic 2

Character/personality

Feel

Same

All right

Dislike

Like

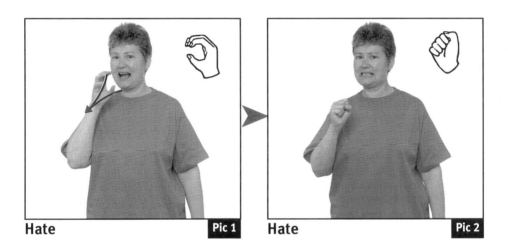

Hate Pic 1 **Hate** Pic 2

Love

Sad

Depressed

Disappointed

Angry

Forgive

Happy Pic 1

Happy Pic 2

162

Careless

Careful

Frustrated Pic 1

Frustrated Pic 2

Cheeky

Aggressive

163

Calm

Afraid

Brave Pic 1

Brave Pic 2

Sly

Honest

Worry

Funny/laugh

Shy

Shy

Embarrassed

Bored

Interesting/interested

Keen

Should/ought to

Shouldn't

Satisfied

Hope

Smile

Envy

True Pic 1

True Pic 2

False Pic 1

False Pic 2

Sure

Correct

Lie (untruth) — Pic 1

Lie (untruth) — Pic 2

Different — Pic 1

Different — Pic 2

Horrible `Pic 1`

Horrible `Pic 2`

Nice

Brilliant

Good

Bad

Worse Pic 1 **Worse** Pic 2

Best Pic 1 **Best** Pic 2

Better **Each**

Alike `Pic 1`

Alike `Pic 2`

Some `Pic 1`

Some `Pic 2`

Many `Pic 1`

Many `Pic 2`

171

More | Pic 1

More | Pic 2

Every

Another/other

Long | Pic 1

Long | Pic 2

Short (in length) A

Short (in height) B

Tall

Small

Big Pic 1

Big Pic 2

173

Tiny

No (naughty) A

No (don't) B

No (not allowed) C

Yes Pic 1

Yes Pic 2

Disagree — Pic 1

Disagree — Pic 2

Agree

Against/object to

Refuse — A Pic 1

Refuse — A Pic 2

Refuse B Pic 1

Refuse B Pic 2

Ugly Pic 1

Ugly Pic 2

Beautiful

Fat

Thin

Perfect

Special

Strange

Ordinary/usual Pic 1

Ordinary/usual Pic 2

Wonderful | Pic 1

Wonderful | Pic 2

Stupid (thing) | Pic 1

Stupid (thing) | Pic 2

Sensitive | Pic 1

Sensitive | Pic 2

Empty `Pic 1`

Empty `Pic 2`

Full (no more space)

Full (of food)

Must

Spoil

Recognise `Pic 1`

Recognise `Pic 2`

Not allowed/forbidden `Pic 1`

Not allowed/forbidden `Pic 2`

Allowed `Pic 1`

Allowed `Pic 2`

Open

Think

Decide A Pic 1

Decide A Pic 2

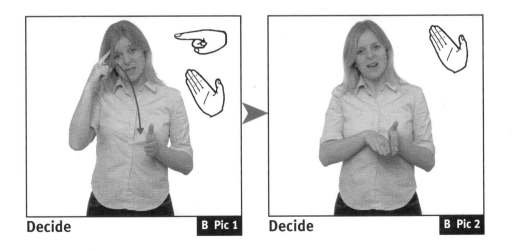

Decide B Pic 1

Decide B Pic 2

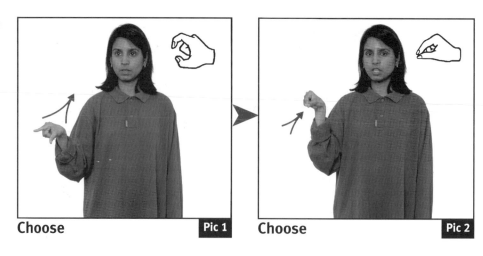

Choose — Pic 1

Choose — Pic 2

Believe — Pic 1

Believe — Pic 2

Don't believe — Pic 1

Don't believe — Pic 2

I know — Pic 1

I know — Pic 2

I don't know — Pic 1

I don't know — Pic 2

Ignore/avoid — Pic 1

Ignore/avoid — Pic 2

Defend

Doubt

Influence

Interrupt

Argue Pic 1

Argue Pic 2

184

Say

Pic 1

Say

Pic 2

Explain DV

Pic 1

Explain DV

Pic 2

Opposite

Pic 1

Opposite

Pic 2

Describing and discussing

185

Can — Pic 1

Can — Pic 2

Cannot

Compare

Won't — Pic 1

Won't — Pic 2

Will

Need

Want

Quick

Slow `Pic 1`

Slow `Pic 2`

Continue — Pic 1

Continue — Pic 2

About (subject)

About (approximately)

Free — Pic 1

Free — Pic 2

Change

Guess

Attitude Pic 1 Attitude Pic 2

Without Pic 1 Without Pic 2

Invite DV — Pic 1

Invite DV — Pic 2

Together — Pic 1

Together — Pic 2

Discuss/talk — Pic 1

Discuss/talk — Pic 2

Seems

Attack/enemy

Criticise DV

War

Trouble `Pic 1`

Trouble `Pic 2`

Young

Old

Dry/thirsty `Pic 1` **Dry/thirsty** `Pic 2`

Soft

Light (weight)

Deep Pic 1

Deep Pic 2

Near

Prefer

Separate Pic 1

Separate Pic 2

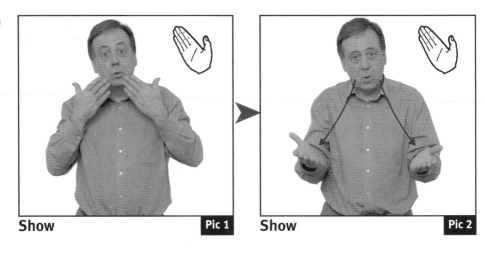

Show — Pic 1

Show — Pic 2

Happen — Pic 1

Happen — Pic 2

Important

Thing

Nearly

News

Before A

Before B

After

Centre

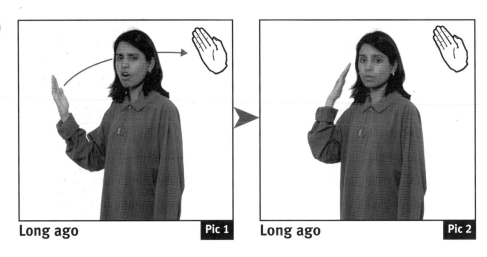

Long ago — Pic 1

Long ago — Pic 2

Now

Soon

Later — Pic 1

Later — Pic 2

196

Again

Often

Sometimes `Pic 1`

Sometimes `Pic 2`

Regular/usually `Pic 1`

Regular/usually `Pic 2`

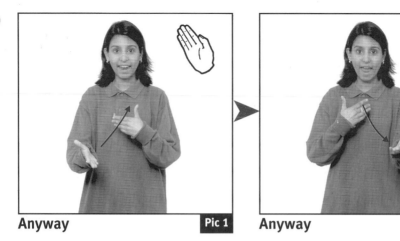

Anyway — Pic 1

Anyway — Pic 2

Just/recently

Maybe

Possibly — Pic 1

Possibly — Pic 2

Always Pic 1

Always Pic 2

Only Pic 1

Only Pic 2

Enough

Both/double

Most — Pic 1

Most — Pic 2

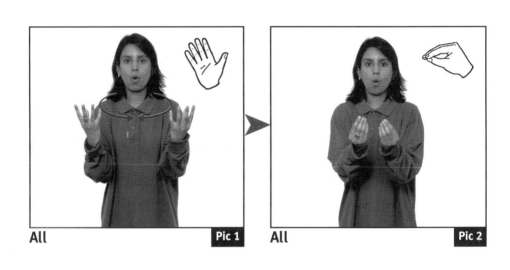

All — Pic 1

All — Pic 2

More (extra)

For/in favour of

Positive

Negative

With

Include

Close/shut `Pic 1`

Close/shut `Pic 2`

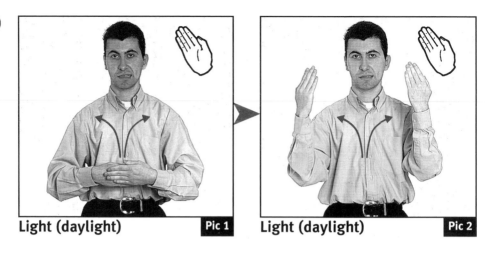

Light (daylight) — Pic 1 Light (daylight) — Pic 2

Stop — Pic 1 Stop — Pic 2

A

B

202

C

D

E

F

G

H

I

J

K

L

M

N

O

P

Q

R

S

T

U

V

W

X

Y

Z

1

2

3

4

5

6

7

8

9

10 Pic 1

10 Pic 2

11

12

13

Use the fingers for 4, 5, 6, 7, 8 and 9 with this hand movement for numbers 14 to 19.

20 `Pic 1` **20** `Pic 2`

100 `Pic 1` **100** `Pic 2`

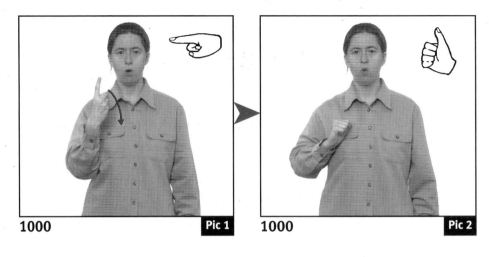

1000 Pic 1

1000 Pic 2

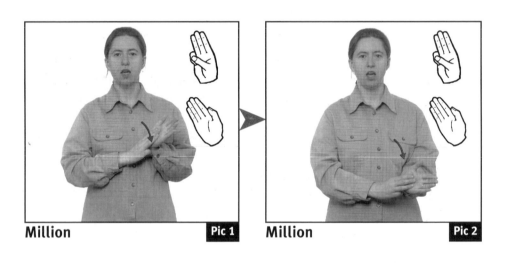

Million Pic 1

Million Pic 2

Useful organisations

If you are interested in finding out more about BSL, these organisations can help:

The Royal National Institute for Deaf People (RNID)
19-23 Featherstone Street, London EC1Y 8SL
Tel: 0808 808 0123 Textphone: 0808 808 9000
Fax: 020 7296 8199
E-mail: informationline@rnid.org.uk
Website: www.rnid.org.uk

RNID has information on most subjects related to deafness and hearing loss. Contact us for a copy of our free publications catalogue. We can also supply details of BSL courses in your area. Ask us for a list, or visit our website.

The British Deaf Association (BDA)
1-3 Worship Street, London EC2A 2AB
Tel: 020 7588 3520 Textphone: 020 7588 3529
Videophone: 020 7374 9065
Fax: 020 7588 3527
E-mail: info@bda.org.uk
Website: www.bda.org.uk

The BDA aims to advance the interests of the Deaf Community and promote greater awareness of their rights and responsibilities. It believes that Deaf people should be enabled, through equal access, to take their full place as members of the wider national community. It provides information and advice, organises conferences, under- takes research, campaigns on issues affecting Deaf people and provides information.

Useful organisations

Council for the Advancement of Communication with Deaf People (CACDP)
Durham University Science Park, Block 4, Stockton Road, Durham DH1 3UZ
Tel: 0191 383 1155 Textphone: 0191 383 7915
Fax: 0191 383 7914
E-mail: durham@cacdp.demon.co.uk
Website: www.cacdp.demon.co.uk

CACDP is the national examining board for communication skills (British Sign Language, Lipspeaking, Deaf Awareness and Deafblind Communication) with deaf people and produces curricula and videos to help students on their courses.

The Forest Bookshop
8 St John Street, Coleford, Gloucestershire GL16 8AR
Tel/Textphone: 01594 833858
Videotelephone: 01594 810637 Bookshop
Fax: 01594 833446
E-mail: deafbooks@forestbooks.com
Website: www.forestbooks.com

The Forest Bookshop specialises in books, videos and CD-ROMs on deafness and deaf issues, keeping over 1,200 titles in stock. They have a fast and efficient mail order service and a free catalogue.

Index of English meanings

C

E

F

T

Y

Notes

Notes

Notes

Notes

Notes

Notes

What is RNID?

The Royal National Institute for Deaf People (RNID) is the largest charity representing the 8.7 million deaf and hard of hearing people in the UK. As a membership charity, we aim to achieve a radically better quality of life for deaf and hard of hearing people. We do this in the following ways:

- Campaigning and lobbying to change laws and government policies.

- Providing information and raising awareness of deafness, hearing loss and tinnitus.

- Training courses and consultancy on deafness and disability.

- Communication services including sign language interpreters.

- Training of interpreters, lipspeakers and speech-to-text operators.

- Seeking lasting change in education for deaf children and young people.

- Employment programmes to help deaf people into work.

- Residential and community services for deaf people with special needs.

- Typetalk, the national telephone relay service for deaf and hard of hearing people.

- Equipment and products for deaf and hard of hearing people.

- Social, medical and technical research.